Nutritious Mushroom Recipes

51 of the world's best easy-to-make wholesome-n-healthy mushroom recipes of STARTERS / SALADS / PIZZAS / SNACKS / VEGGIES / SOUPS

By
Prabhjot Mundhir

Photographs by
Sanjay Jadhav

Pustak Mahal®
Delhi • Bangalore • Mumbai
• Patna • Hyderabad

Publishers
Pustak Mahal, Delhi-110006

Sales Centres
- 6686, Khari Baoli, Delhi-110006, *Ph:* 23944314, 23911979
- 10-B, Netaji Subhash Marg, Daryaganj, New Delhi-110002
  Ph: 23268292, 23268293, 23279900 · *Fax:* 011-23280567
  E-mail: rapidexdelhi@indiatimes.com

Administrative Office
J-3/16 (Opp. Happy School), Daryaganj, New Delhi-110002
Ph: 23276539, 23272783, 23272784 · *Fax:* 011-23260518
E-mail: info@pustakmahal.com
Website: www.pustakmahal.com

Branch Offices
BANGALORE: 22/2, Mission Road (Shama Rao's Compound),
Bangalore-560027
Ph: 22234025 · *Fax:* 080-22240209
E-mail: pmblr@sancharnet.in · pustak@sancharnet.in
MUMBAI: 23-25, Zaoba Wadi (Opp. VIP Showroom),
Thakurdwar, Mumbai-400002,
Ph: 22010941 · *Fax:* 022-22053387
E-mail: rapidex@bom5.vsnl.net.in
PATNA: Khemka House, 1st Floor
(Opp. Women's Hospital), Ashok Rajpath,
Patna-800004 · *Telefax:* 0612-2302719/3094193
E-mail: rapidexptn@rediffmail.com
HYDERABAD: 5-1-707/1, Brij Bhawan, Bank Street, Koti,
Hyderabad-500095,
Ph: 24737530 · *Fax:* 040-24737290
E-mail: pustakmahalhyd@yahoo.co.in

© **Pustak Mahal, 6686, Khari Baoli, Delhi-110006**

ISBN 81-223-0893-7

Edition : January 2005

Printed at: Param Offsetters, Okhla, New Delhi-110020.

Contents

Preface

"From food do all creatures come into being," says the ***Bhagavat Gita.*** But to keep oneself fully fit and functional, it requires proper understanding of the body, sound health, proper eating practices and disciplined living. Here, food plays a vital role. 'Food can make or break you' because, as the legend goes, *you are what you eat.* Although every community in India has a distinct food ethos, most of these, however, have been influenced by Aryan beliefs and practices. References given about the food the Harappans ate are actually based on archaeological artifacts, but the food eaten by the Aryans are documented by literary works starting with the *Rig Veda* of about 1500 BC.

Over a period of time, Indian cookery has been influenced by the cooking styles of various people of different faiths who made India their home. Then known and unknown master chefs of each age experimented with different ingredients by way of different combinations and cooking techniques according to the growing needs of their time.

Although the mushroom – one of nature's greatest wonder foods – has already found its place of pride in the kitchens of the educated and the elite all over the world, in India it is yet to be commonly used by all and sundry in everyday meals, as it was not easily available until now. Today, with its cultivation all over the country and increasing appearance in supermarkets and daily bazaars, it has become easily available and affordable too. Its irresistible taste, exotic flavour and aroma attract food lovers. As a result, the mushroom's delicious dishes are becoming a healthy alternative to meat dishes in many gatherings.

Counting the benefits of this wonderful health food, especially keeping the Indian taste and requirements in mind, I have tried to develop and innovate a few easy-to-follow recipes with this versatile ingredient for our daily diet because fresh mushrooms are an attractive addition to any vegetarian or non-vegetarian dish.*

The book contains recipes on **Starters, Soups, Salads and dishes for the Main Course**. Some of the starters and the quick stir-fried vegetable dishes of mushrooms are just ideal for the tiffin boxes of growing children, working ladies and other office-goers. Stir-fried mixed vegetables are not only exceptionally tasty and nutritious with their natural goodness, but their contrasting flavours, textures – both crunchy and soft – and the pleasing variety of colours and shapes are also visually appealing. Special care has been taken to ensure that more and more users become mushroom friendly. Therefore, most ingredients used for preparing the dishes are common ones easily available at home. To retain the natural taste and flavour, spices are used sparingly as a good cook knows that spices do not make the dish special but the right use of ingredients in the right proportion, the cooking technique and aesthetic presentation turn an ordinary dish into an extraordinary one. All the recipes are tried and tested, so anyone who knows the basics of cooking can master the art of using mushrooms in everyday meals. Moreover, these dishes can easily be a part of any Indian or Continental menu set for special occasions too.

In short, mushrooms used in everyday cooking will help maintain the good health of your loved ones.

---

* Each dish featured in this book serves 4 to 6 persons.

Acknowledgement

I would like to thank my family, friends and well-wishers for their unrelenting support.

Introduction

An ancient nutritional delicacy is actually one of nature's **wonder foods**. It is not a vegetable, a nut, a seed, an animal, a fruit or a grain. It manufactures no green chlorophyll, needs no sunlight, and yet grows with great rapidity. Some varieties are known to have anti-cholesterol and antibiotic properties. The common variety is full of protein of high quality as well as B vitamins. Therefore, it is considered one of the best **health foods**.

Earlier, mushrooms only grew naturally but now they are cultivated all over the world. In India, Kashmiri guchchi is one of the rare examples of nature's bounty. Despite great efforts made all over the world, guchchi still grows naturally and, therefore, is an exorbitantly expensive vegetarian item. In Kashmir itself, it is sold for five thousand rupees a kilogram. Mushrooms are also used in certain medicines.

Did you know?

One cannot even imagine the bounty that a mushroom contains:

- It contains the anti-stress vitamin **pantothenicad B-5**. This vitamin keeps the bodily process running smoothly in the face of terrific shocks to the system. It is also important for the production of anti-bodies to protect against infection and has been used with great success to minimise allergic reactions. The mushroom is a great storehouse of vitamin B-5, more than any other plant food.

- Mushrooms are also a great storehouse of the **B-3** vitamin known as **niacin** – among numerous other protective roles, it keeps cholesterol levels in check and promotes the well-being of the central nervous system, including mental health.

- Generous amounts of **riboflavin B-2** are found in mushrooms. Vitamin B-2 is needed to spark many vital enzyme reactions to help keep the skin looking youthful and healthy, and is needed to repair injuries.
- Mushrooms also contain useful amounts of **thiamine B-1** vitamin and **pyridoxine B-6** vitamin, which are excellent sources of blood building elements since they contain a good amount of iron and copper.
- Among the nutritional advantages of mushrooms are high contents of glutamic acid and amino acids, which are very essential for proper functioning of the brain. Dr Paul C Brag – an anti-ageing specialist – says, "On one of my hiking trips in Canada, I was stranded in the north woods where I lived 17 days in good health on wild mushrooms. I never lost my energy because mushrooms contain many vitamins and minerals as well as splendid protein, fats and carbohydrates."

Some historical facts about mushrooms

a. The mushroom is an ancient nutritional delicacy.
b. Egyptian legends claim the mushroom was the plant of immortality.
c. A Japanese legend says a certain variety of mushroom prolongs life.
d. The ancient Chinese believed it was an aphrodisiac.
e. The epicures of Rome and the royalty of Britain and France permitted only the courts and palaces to serve mushrooms.
f. Advanced civilisations in many parts of the world in Mexico, Central America, Russia, Greece, China and Egypt practised mushroom rituals.

g. Many believed the mushroom contained properties that would confer the ability to find lost objects, heal the sick, produce supernatural strength and aid the soul in reaching the realm of gods.

h. The ancient Iranian Aryans and the early Vedic Aryans believed that the famous *somras* was made from some kind of mushroom. It was known as the 'Soma plant'. This exhilarating drink was commonly offered to gods and imbibed by the priests and proponents of sacrifice. It was clearly distinguished from a mere alcoholic stimulant. There is a reference in the *Rig Veda* that an individual who imbibed *somras* was exhilarated beyond his natural powers and the juice itself was described as being primeval, all powerful, healing all diseases, bestower of riches, loved by the gods, even by the Supreme Being. The god Indra was exhorted to destroy enemy strongholds after fortifying himself with Soma juice.

i. The *Rig Veda* has documented food and food habits of yesteryears very well. Earlier, mushrooms grew naturally and no planned cultivation took place. Therefore, only royalty consumed mushrooms worldwide.

The Recipes

Mushroom Salads

Of all the good foods nature has given us, mushrooms are one of the greatest wonder foods. We should include mushrooms in our daily diet in one form or the other to maintain good health. Mushrooms are delicious both raw and cooked. Fresh mushrooms are an attractive addition to any vegetarian or non-vegetarian dish. Sliced or halved mushrooms absorb the aroma of dressings, gravies, curries or masalas nicely because of their spongy texture and then distribute it evenly to the entire preparation. The subtle delicate aroma of this wonder food makes the dish special. Since the simplest and most nutritious way to eat mushrooms is in the raw form, sliced mushrooms combined with other vegetables make excellent salads.

1) Mushrooms can be combined with leafy and green vegetables. Mushroom slices can be mixed with raw finely shredded spinach, lettuce, cabbage and spring onions with greens, cubed cucumbers, carrots, radishes, tomatoes, red, green and yellow peppers and chopped coriander and chillies. Bean sprouts and boiled corn too add taste to the salad dish.

2) Button mushrooms can be combined for salads with boiled flowerets of broccoli and cauliflower, green peas and beans, boiled fresh potatoes, cubed cottage cheese and skinned cubed tomatoes etc.

3) Raw mushroom slices can be mixed with omelette stripes, boiled shredded chicken or salamis, boiled pasta and parsley along with other vegetables.

4) Raw mushrooms taste extremely good along with cubed apples, pears and pineapple cubes simply sprinkled with lemon dressing.

5) Even soaked and revived dry fruits like cashew nuts, walnuts, almonds or simple peanuts and raisins sparingly combined with mushrooms make delicious salad.

Note

You may use any dressing like lemon dressing, French dressing, mustard sauce or cheese cream dressing etc., but the mushrooms should be mixed with the dressing some time before actual consumption, so that they absorb the extra flavour.

Avoid

Too much salt in the salads. Mushrooms contain natural salts.

Mushroom and Corn Salad

Ingredients

Mushrooms	200 gm	Tomatoes	2 nos
Corn kernels	100 gm	Cabbage leaves	6 nos
Spring onions	3 nos	Lettuce	8 leaves
Cucumber	1 large	French dressing	¼ cup

Preparation

For French Dressing

Mix together 2 tbsp table vinegar, 1 tsp salt, 1 tsp sugar, ½ tsp pepper powder, ¼ tsp mustard powder and 1 tsp olive oil or any other refined cooking oil in a bottle and shake well. Refrigerate till required.

1) Remove the spine of cabbage leaves and two lettuce leaves. Roll them tightly and shred very finely. Immerse in cold water to keep them crisp.
2) Slice tomatoes, cucumber and washed mushrooms.
3) Chop spring onions.
4) Place sliced mushrooms, corn kernels and spring onions in a bowl and pour the dressing on top and refrigerate.
5) Drain the shredded cabbage and lettuce. Keep them in a refrigerator. Assemble with mushroom mixture before eating.

Serving

For assembling the salads *careful carelessness* is required.

Take a big platter and spread the crisp cabbage leaves over it. Place the lettuce the way you like. Make one circle of tomato slices and another one with cucumber slices. In the centre of the platter place the mushroom and corn mixture. Pour the leftover dressing on top and serve cold.

Variation

- Chop tomatoes, cucumber and cabbage too and mix with mushroom mixture and serve on bed of lettuce only.
- Instead of corn, use boiled bean or moong sprouts or even green peas.
- Add chopped chicken salamis.
- Add boiled cauliflower or broccoli to the mushrooms and spring onions.
- Add shredded carrots or cubed radishes.
- Sprinkle the salad with roasted sesame seeds, roasted and pounded peanuts or black pepper etc.

Preparatory Time: 15 mins

Cheese Cream Mushroom Salad

Ingredients

Mushrooms	200 gm	Green or red pepper	1 no.
Cucumber	2 nos	Lettuce leaves	8 nos
Apples	2 nos	Juice of lemon	1 tbsp
Pineapple slices	4 nos	Cheese cream dressing	1 cup plus
Boiled potato	1 no. large	Fresh cream (optional)	¼ cup
Spring onions	4 nos		

Preparation

For Cheese Cream Dressing

Mix together 1 cup hung curd, 1 tsp cooking oil, 2 tsp white pepper powder, 1 tsp sugar, 1 tsp salt and 1 tsp mustard powder. Mix properly and chill before use.

1) Immerse the lettuce leaves in cold water.

2) Peel the apples and cut them into one-inch pieces and smear with lemon juice to avoid discoloration. Cube the pineapple slices and boiled potato too and mix with the apples.

3) Wash the mushrooms, spring onions and green or red pepper. Cut mushrooms into halves. Chop the spring onions and pepper too.

4) Now mix prepared fruits and vegetables together in a bowl and add the chilled dressing. Add fresh chilled cream too for the rich and creamer taste. Mix gently and refrigerate till used.

Serving

In a platter arrange the lettuce leaves and then place the cheese cream salad in the centre. Serve cold.

Variation

- Use fresh pears instead of apples.
- Mix some fried bread croutons with the salad just before serving.
- Instead of cheesse cream dressing you may use mayonnaise sauce as a base.

Preparatory Time: 30 mins

Mushroom and Pasta Salad

Ingredients

Mushroom	200 gm	Lettuce	8 leaves
Boiled macaroni	2 cups	Tomato sauce	¼ cup
Boiled potatoes	2 nos	Mayonnaise	½ cup
Cucumber	1 large	Mustard sauce	¼ cup
Carrots	2 nos	Celery sticks	2 nos
Boiled green peas	1 cup	Fresh cream	¼ cup
Red pepper	1 no.	(optional)	

Preparation

1) Cut mushrooms into halves.
2) Dice potatoes and one cucumber.
3) Cut red pepper and carrots in matchstick fashion.
4) Chop celery very fine.
5) Remove the spine of cabbage leaves and roll them tightly. Shred them fine and soak in cold water for half an hour. Drain and keep cool.
6) Slice one cucumber very thinly without peeling for greener effect.

Assembling

Mix all the chopped ingredients together. Pour the sauces over. Mix gently with a light hand and refrigerate salad for at least 30 minutes before serving.

Serving

On a large platter arrange the cooled cabbage and then place mixed salad in the centre. Decorate with slices of cucumber. Even onion rings and tomato slices can be used for this purpose.

Preparatory Time: 30 mins

Spinach and Mushroom Soup

Ingredients

Mushrooms	1 cup (chopped)		Butter	1 tsp
Spinach	2 cups (leaves and stems chopped)		Ginger	1-inch piece (grated)
			Peppercorn	10 nos
Tomatoes	3 nos (chopped)		Bay leaf	1 no.
			Black cardamoms	2 nos
Onion	1 nos		Sesame seeds	1 tbsp (roasted)
Mushrooms	4 nos (sliced)		or	
Cream	4 tsp		Garlic	1 tbsp (chopped)
Corn flour	2 tbsp			

Cooking

1) Boil everything together for the first 10 minutes and then simmer for 45 minutes.
2) Strain and collect the soup. Pass the vegetables through the mixer.
3) Mix with the soup and strain once again. Heat soup, bring it to boiling point.
4) Mix corn flour with a little water and add to the soup. Boil till the soup thickens.
5) Heat butter, fry garlic in it till just pink, and add to the soup. Or sprinkle the roasted sesame seeds.

Serving

In every soup bowl (with each serving) slice one mushroom each and add 1 tsp cream to the soup and serve hot with any crisp bread or soup sticks.

Avoid

Adding salt to the soup.

Note

In this soup no salt is added because spinach and mushrooms contain natural salts.

Preparatory Time: 25 mins

Chicken Mushroom Soup

Ingredients

Carrot	1 sliced	Water	6 cups
Bay leaf	1 no.	Almond blanched	6 nos
Chicken breast	1 no.	Cream (optional)	¼ cup
Celery	1 stalk	White sauce	1 cup
Onion	1 sliced	Peppercorns	10 nos
Rice	¼ cup	Salt	To taste
Mushroom sliced	1¼ cup		

Cooking

1) Mix together celery, onions, water, carrot, chicken and peppercorns.
2) Boil and then simmer for 45 minutes. Strain.
3) Wash rice and add to the stock.
4) Bring to boil and then simmer till rice is tender.
5) Lift chicken and slice or shred it.
6) Now add shredded chicken and sliced mushrooms to the stock. Boil.
7) Mix white sauce gently and boil the soup for 2 minutes.
8) Remove and check the seasonings. Add cream.

Serving

Serve soup garnished with blenched almond slivers.

Note

This soup combines very well with garlic bread and any fruit salad. It makes a complete meal.

Preparatory Time: 1 hour

Mushroom Frankies with Enchilda Sauce

Ingredients

For the Frankies

Whole wheat flour	2 cups
Milk	½ cup
Oil	1 tbsp
Salt	½ tsp
Water for making dough	

For Stuffing

Mushrooms sliced	3 cups
Onions sliced	1 cup
Cheese grated	1 cup
Coriander chopped	¼ cup
Green chillies chopped	3 nos
Oil	2 tbsp
Seasonings	

For Enchilda Sauce

Chilli powder	3 tbsp
Tomato sauce	1½ cup
Cooking oil	3 tbsp
Yellow corn meal	1½ tbsp

For Coating

Eggs	4 nos
Milk	½ cup
Pepper powder	1 tsp
Salt	½ tsp
Oil for frying	

Preparation and Cooking

1) Mix all ingredients for the frankies and make a pliable dough. Knead it well so that it can be rolled nicely. Divide dough into lemon-sized balls. Roll each ball into a thin chapatti and cook on a griddle (tava).

2) Heat oil and sauté sliced onions and mushrooms. Add coriander, green chillies and seasonings. Keep aside.

3) Heat 3 tbsp cooking oil and add yellow corn meal. Brown corn meal and add chilli powder, tomato sauce and salt to taste. Cook for 10–15 minutes on slow fire and remove.

4) Heat heavy bottomed pan and pour 1 tsp oil. Lower heat.

5) Beat eggs with milk, salt and pepper. Dip 1 chapatti at a time in it and place on the pan. Turn the side of the chapatti and place 1 tbsp mushroom stuffing on it. Sprinkle some cheese over it and roll it. In this way, finish with all the chapattis and the stuffing.

Serving

Place the cooked frankies in a serving plate and spread 1 tsp Enchilda sauce on each of them lengthwise. Serve hot. You may dip the rolled chapatti in the sauce and enjoy it.

Note

Enchilda sauce is a Mexican relish to be eaten with Tortillas.

Tip

Even leftover chapattis or phulkas can be used to make these Frankies.

Preparatory Time: 40 mins

Mushroom Chowder

Ingredients

Mushrooms	1 cup sliced	Spring onions	2 nos (with greens finely chopped)
American corn	1 cup		
Red pepper	1 no. small	Corn flour	3 tbsp (mixed in a little water)
Green pepper	1 small (cut in matchstick style)		
		Parsley	1 tbsp chopped
Tomato	1 large (skinned, cut in cubes)	Water	6 cups
		Salt	To taste

Preparation

1) Boil everything except parsley and corn flour for 10 minutes.
2) Add cornstarch and mix well. Boil.
3) Remove and check the seasonings.

Serving

Serve hot with any bread and non-vegetarian dish.

Note

Chowder: A thick soup or stew made of fish and various vegetables.

Preparatory Time: 20 mins

Mushroom and Spinach Souffle

Ingredients

Spinach (finely chopped)	2 cups/ 200 gm	Milk	1½ cup
Butter (for greasing)	3 tbsp +	Eggs	4 separated
		Pepper (freshly ground)	1 tsp
Garlic clove (crushed)	1 no.	Nutmeg (grated)	¼ tsp
Mushrooms	200 gm	Cheese (grated)	2 tbsp
Flour	2 tbsp	Salt	To taste

Preparation

1) Pre-heat the oven to 190 degrees centigrade.
2) Chop spinach and cook over moderate heat for 5 minutes. Transfer to a strainer and keep it under running water to cool. Drain and squeeze properly.
3) Slice mushrooms.
4) Heat butter and add mushrooms to it. Cook till all the liquid is evaporated. Add spinach and mix well. Cover and keep warm.
5) Boil 1 cup milk. In a separate bowl mix egg yolks and flour. Mix it with electric hand beater. Pour milk into the egg and flour mixture and mix well. Transfer mixture into the pan and simmer on slow fire to thicken.
6) Remove from fire. Mix with the spinach and mushroom mixture. Season it with salt, pepper and nutmeg.
7) Butter a soufflé dish and sprinkle grated cheese on the sides. Keep aside. Save some cheese.
8) Whisk the egg whites stiff.
9) Fold it into the spinach mixture and turn it into the soufflé dish. Spread well and sprinkle the rest of the cheese on top.

Baking

Bake in the hot oven for about 30 to 40 minutes or until golden in colour. Serve hot with any Continental meal.

Preparatory Time: 1 hour

Stir-fried Peppers and Mushroom

Ingredients

Green peppers (capsicums)	3 nos sliced	Pepper powder	1 tsp
Red pepper	1 no. sliced	Vinegar/lemon juice	1 tbsp
Yellow pepper	1 no. sliced	Soya sauce/ salt + sugar	1 tsp
Mushrooms sliced	2 cups/ 250 gm		
Ginger	1-inch pieces thinly sliced	Cooking oil	2-3 tbsp
		Mustard seeds	1 tsp

Cooking

1) Heat oil and crackle mustard seeds. Add green peppers and stir-fry for 2–3 mins, remove and keep aside.

2) In the same oil now put the red pepper and yellow peppers. Stir-fry for 2–3 minutes.

3) Now add sliced mushrooms and stir. Mix green peppers too, and stir-fry till dry.

4) Now add black pepper powder, vinegar and soya sauce.

5) Mix well and serve hot.

Note

No salt is added to this colourfully crunchy dish.

This preparation is just ideal to be carried in the lunch box.

Preparatory Time: 10 mins

Mushroom Stuffed Tomatoes

Ingredients

Large tomatoes (firm but ripe)	6 nos		Coriander (finely chopped)	½ cup
Mushrooms (finely chopped)	1 cup		Plain boiled rice	1 cup
Onion (finely chopped)	1 large		Cheese (grated)	3 tbsp
Ginger (grated)	2-inch piece		Bread slices	2 big
			Oil	3 tbsp
Green chillies (finely chopped)	4 nos		Cumin seeds	½ tsp
			Garam masala	½ tsp
Black pepper powder (optional)	1 tsp		Butter	1 tbsp
			Salt	To taste

Preparation

1) Wash and dry tomatoes. Scoop them with peeler or a teaspoon. Keep the pulp aside. Now sprinkle the inside of tomatoes with salt generously and invert so that all the water drains and the shells of tomatoes are ready to be filled. Invert for at least one hour.

2) Heat the oven.

Cooking

1) Heat oil, crackle cumin and add onions to be fried. Crisp fry the onions and add tomato pulp, ginger, green chilli, salt, pepper and garam masala. Cook tomato pulp till the oil almost separates.

2) Add rice and mix well. Add chopped coriander and cheese. Mix properly. Cool mixture.

3) Break bread slices and put them in a mixer for making fresh crumbs.

4) Now stuff tomatoes with the mixture and sprinkle the top of the tomatoes with fresh breadcrumbs.

5) Now dot the tops with butter.

Baking

Bake the tomatoes in a hot oven for half an hour.

Serving

Serve hot with any Indian or Continental food.

Note

If you don't eat chillies you may add extra black pepper and omit green chillies.

Variation

- Instead of tomatoes, use capsicums.
- Instead of rice, use boiled noodles or even shredded chicken or mutton mince.

Preparatory Time: 40 mins

Stir-fried Mushroom, Methi and Moong Sprouts

Ingredients

Mushrooms	200 gm shredded	Garlic chopped	1 tbsp
		Cumin seeds	1 tsp
Methi leaves	1 cup (washed and cleaned)	Pepper powder	1 tsp
		Tomatoes	2 nos
		Oil	3–4 tbsp
Moong sprouts	1 cup	Salt	To taste
Chilli-garlic	1 tbsp		

Cooking

1) Burn tomatoes on gas flame and remove the skin. Halve tomatoes and slice lengthwise.

2) Heat oil, crackle cumin seeds in it.

3) Add methi leaves and fry for 2 minutes.

4) Add moong sprouts and fry for another 2 minutes.

5) Add chilli-garlic sauce, black pepper and salt.

6) Add sliced mushrooms and stir-fry for another 2 minutes.

7) Lastly add sliced tomatoes and stir-fry for 2 minutes. Remove to a serving dish when the dish is dry.

Serving

Serve hot with dal and rice.

You may enjoy this dish with paranthas too.

Preparatory Time: 10 mins

Mushroom Surprise Sandwich

Ingredients

Brown bread	8 slices	Sliced fresh mushroom	4 nos
Mayonnaise	¼ cup	Cheese slices	4 nos
or		Tomato slices	From 2 tomatoes
Fresh green chutney mixed with butter and mushroom sauce	1 cup	Lettuce leaves	4 nos
Chilli-garlic (optional)	¼ cup	Sesame seeds roasted	3 tbsp

Preparation

1) Crisp bread lightly in a toaster.

2) Apply mayonnaise or fresh green chutney on two toasts. Apply chilli garlic too if you are using it.

3) Spread one lettuce leaf on a toast and arrange tomato slices and sprinkle sesame seeds on it.

4) Now arrange cheese slice and then sliced mushrooms.

5) Cover it with another toast and wrap it in kitchen foil. This way make 4 sets. Use as and when required.

Variation

• You may add sliced peppers or cucumber instead of tomatoes. You may sprinkle it with sprouts instead of sesame seeds.

• If you are a non-vegetarian, instead of cheese slice, add salamis or a slice of meat loaf or even a thin omelette. Then follow rest of the recipe. With a little imagination you can prepare a variety of sandwiches.

• Such sandwiches are meals within themselves because they have the nutrients, especially protein, for good health. You may consume some light salad like Coleslaw with them.

Preparatory Time: 15 mins

Stir-fried Mushroom, Cauliflower, Capsicums, Babycorn and Carrots

Ingredients

Mushrooms	200 gm	Dry peanut chutney with red chilli	2 tbsp
Carrots	2 nos	Coriander (optional)	Chopped
Capsicum	1 large	Cooking oil	3 tbsp
Baby corn	10 nos	Dry red chilli (whole)	2 nos
Cauliflower	1 small		
Mustard seeds	1 tsp	Salt	To taste

Preparation

1) Wash and cut mushrooms into halves.
2) Peel and cut carrots into a fancy shape.
3) De-seed the capsicum and cut into 1-inch cubes.
4) Break cauliflower into small flowerets and soak in salted water.

Cooking

1) Boil carrots and cauliflower flowerets for 5 minutes.
2) Heat oil and add whole chillies. When black in colour remove and discard it. Crackle mustard in the same oil.
3) Add boiled cauliflower, baby corn and cubed capsicum to the hot oil. Stir-fry on high fire for 2 minutes.
4) Add mushrooms, salt and pepper.
5) Stir for another 2 minutes and then add carrots and leftover liquid. Fry for another minute.
6) Add 2 tsp dry peanut chutney and coriander together.
7) Mix well and remove.

Serving

Serve hot with *varan-bhat* or dal and rice preparation.

Preparatory Time: 20 mins

Mushroom Slaw

Ingredients

Mushrooms	200 gm	Pears	2 nos
Cabbage leaves	8 nos	Lemon dressing	3 tbsp
Walnuts	1 cup	Tomato	1 large
Oranges	3 nos		

Preparation

For Lemon Dressing

Mix together juice of 2 lemons, 1 tsp salt, 1 tsp white pepper powder, ¼ tsp mustard powder and 1 tsp sugar. Mix well and chill before use.

1) Cut mushrooms into slices and mix with the lemon dressing. Keep aside under refrigeration.

2) Remove the spine of cabbage leaves, roll them tight and shred very finely. Soak in cold water for some time. Drain and keep cool.

3) Peel oranges and chop the segments after removing the seeds.

4) Soak walnuts. When dry fruits are soaked for five to six hours, they are revived and easier to digest. Chop them.

5) Remove the pith and cut pears in matchstick fashion. Immediately mix with mushrooms to avoid discoloration.

6) Cut the large tomato into thin slices for decorating the salad dish.

Assembling

Mix together all the chopped ingredients (except tomato rings) and mushroom mixture and place in a flat dish. Arrange slices on the outer edges and serve.

Variation

You may use sweet orange segments instead of oranges and soaked cashew nuts or peanuts instead of walnuts. Even black grapes make an interesting substitute and add colour to the dish.

Note

If you find the salad too sweet due to the fruits, you may add ½ cup chopped spring onions to the dish.

Preparatory Time: 10 mins

Mushroom Cooked Chinese Style (Mushroom Chowmein)

Ingredients

Mushrooms (halved)	200 gm	Pepper	1 tsp
		Chilli powder	1 tsp
Sprouts	1 cup	Ginger-garlic paste	2 tbsp
Capsicums (green, cut in cubes)	½ cup	Corn flour	2 tbsp
		Water	3 cups
Red pepper (cut in cubes)	½ cup	Red chillies (whole)	2 nos
Tomatoes (skinned and cubed)	1½ cup	Oil	3 tbsp
		Soya sauce	2 tbsp
Spring onions	6 nos	Crisp fried noodles	For 4 servings
Onion greens, finely chopped	½ cup	Chicken shreds (optional)	½ cup

Cooking

1) Heat oil and put chillies in it. Remove once they are black. They impart flavour to the oil. When you cook in chilli oil, the food has an absolutely different taste.

2) Add spring onions and sauté. Add ginger-garlic paste. Put both peppers in it and stir for a minute. Now add sprouts and fry for another couple of minutes.

3) Add chopped tomatoes and rest of the ingredients. Stir well. Add water and bring to boil. Cook on high flame for 3 minutes.

4) Mix corn flour with a little water and mix with the boiling vegetables and cook till the dish attains a body and has a glaze.

Serving

Serve hot with boiled/fried rice or noodles.

Note

For making Fried Noodles, half boil noodles, drain and rinse. Cool. Deep-fry them in small portions till crisp. Drain on paper, cool and store.

Preparatory Time: 20 mins

Buttered Broccoli and Mushroom

Ingredients

Mushrooms halved	2 cups	Garlic minced	1 tbsp
Broccoli flowerets	2 cups	Crushed pepper corns	1 tbsp
Red pepper	1 small	Lemon juice	1 tbsp
Butter	2 tbsp	Sesame seeds	2 tbsp

Preparation

1) Boil the broccoli in just enough water to make it tender but crisp or microwave it for 5 minutes in a dish covered with a lid. Add a pinch of salt to the water while cooking.

2) Cut red pepper in matchstick fashion.

3) Dry fry the sesame seeds. Keep aside.

Cooking

1) Heat butter in a heavy bottomed pan and put minced garlic in it. Stir. Add crushed peppercorns too, so that the pepper imparts its aroma.

2) Add halved mushrooms and stir-fry for 2 minutes.

3) Now add broccoli and stir constantly but carefully. Cover the dish for 2 minutes, so that the broccoli absorbs the garlic-pepper aroma properly.

4) Open the dish and add red pepper and lemon juice. Mix lightly.

Serving

Transfer the cooked dish into a serving dish and sprinkle sesame seeds on top and serve hot.

Preparatory Time: 15 mins

Mushroom Kebabs

Ingredients

Mushrooms (chopped)	200 gm	Breadcrumbs	2 tbsp
Chana dal	½ cup	Sesame seeds	To roll the kebabs
Onion (chopped)	1 no.	Fresh mint (chopped)	2 tbsp
Garlic	2 cloves	Garam masala	1 tsp
Ginger (grated)	1-inch piece	Salt	To taste
Green chillies (chopped)	2 nos	Red chilli powder	Optional
Potato (boiled and mashed)	1 no.	Mushrooms (sliced)	4 nos
		Oil for frying	

Cooking

1) Soak chana dal for 1 hour and then boil. Add ginger, garlic and onion to it before boiling.

2) Cook mushrooms separately.

3) Dry grind cooked dal and mushroom together.

4) Now mix ground dal-mushroom mixture with mashed potatoes, ginger, chilli, breadcrumbs, mint, garam masala and salt. If using red chilli, add it at this point.

5) Divide dough into 12 balls. Take one ball and flatten a bit and place one slice of mushroom in the centre. Shape it like a thick cutlet or shape it like a mushroom. In this way, place one piece of sliced mushroom in all the patties.

6) Now spread sesame seeds in a plate and roll all the patties lightly with these aromatic seeds.

7) Heat oil and fry kebabs in it. Drain them on the kitchen paper/paper napkins.

Serving

Serve hot with chutney/sauce and salads. These can be served as good starters.

Preparatory Time: 30 mins

Spicy Mushroom

Ingredients

Mushrooms	200 gm	Onion (chopped)	1 large
Curds fresh	1 cup/ 200 gm	Gram flour or	
Ginger (finely chopped)	1 tsp	Roasted, powdered chana dal	1 tbsp
Chilli-garlic	1 tsp	Roasted peanut powder	1 tbsp
Turmeric powder	½ tsp		
Salt	To taste	Cooking oil/butter	2 tbsp
Coriander (chopped)	½ cup	Mustard seeds	½ tsp
		Peppercorns	4 nos
Green peas (boiled)	½ cup (optional)	Cloves	4 nos
		Cinnamon	½-inch stick

Cooking

1) Heat oil and add whole spices so that they impart their flavour.

2) Now add mustard seeds. Crackle them and add chopped onion. Fry to pinkish colour.

3) Add chopped ginger and half the coriander and stir-fry.

4) Add gram flour or chana dal powder and fry till it is golden. Now add beaten curds, chilli-garlic sauce, salt and turmeric powder.

5) Add mushrooms and cook on low heat for 5–10 minutes or till the gravy is semi-solid in texture.

6) Remove and garnish with the remaining coriander.

Serving

Serve hot with hot phulka or parantha.

Preparatory Time: 30 mins

Stuffed Mushroom

Ingredients

Large mushrooms (stem removed)	16 nos	Fresh mint (finely chopped)	2 tbsp
Onion (finely chopped)	1 no.	or	
		Dry mint powder	1 tsp
Stems of mushrooms – chopped		Egg	1 no.
		Cheese (grated)	2 tbsp
Chicken salamis (finely chopped)	4 nos	Butter	1 tbsp
		Pepper powder	½ tsp

Preparation

1) Mix 2 tbsp vinegar + 1 tsp oil + one pinch salt + ½ tsp pepper powder + a pinch mustard powder.

48

With a peeler carefully make a depression in mushrooms. Properly brush mushrooms inside and outside with vinegar mixture and keep aside.

2) Heat oven.

Cooking

1) Heat oil and sauté onion and green chillies.
2) Add chopped mushrooms and stir-fry for a minute.
3) Add chopped salamis.
4) Beat egg and add to the mixture. Just curdle it and remove from fire.
5) Now add 1 tbsp grated cheese, fresh mint and pepper powder. Mix well. The stuffing should be nice and soft.
6) Stuff mushroom caps carefully and sprinkle the tops with cheese.
7) Bake in hot oven for 15–20 minutes.

Serving

Serve hot.

Note

1) This preparation is a good starter.
2) If you want to avoid egg, use fresh breadcrumbs from 1 large slice.
3) You can use parsley/coriander instead of mint.

Preparatory Time: 30 mins

Mushroom Stuffed Potato Balls

Ingredients

Potatoes	4 large	Ajwain	½ tsp
Mushrooms	250 gm	Mango powder	½ tsp
Mint	2 tbsp chopped	Red chilli powder	½ tsp
		Garam masala	½ tsp
Spring onions with greens	4 nos	Sesame seeds	½ cup
		Butter	½ tbsp
Moong sprouts	¼ cup	Oil	2 tbsp
Green chillies	4 nos	Salt	To taste

Preparation and Cooking

1) Peel, wash and boil potatoes. Mash when still hot. Keep aside to cool.

2) Chop spring onions, green chillies and mushrooms very finely.

3) Roast half the sesame seeds and pound coarsely.

4) Heat oil, crackle ajwain seeds, add chopped onions and green chillies and sauté. Add chopped mushrooms and sprouts. Stir-fry for a couple of minutes. Now add salt and other dry ingredients. Mix well. Add chopped mint and remove from fire. Sprinkle roasted sesame seeds, mix and cool the stuffing.

5) Put the oven on.

6) Add butter and a pinch of salt to the mashed and cooled potatoes and knead well till potatoes have no lumps.

7) Divide potato mixture and mushroom stuffing into equal parts. Flatten one part potato dough on your palm and place one part stuffing in the centre and roll it into a ball properly and keep aside. Finish all portions the same way. Now spread the rest of the sesame seeds in a plate and roll all the potato balls gently.

8) Place balls on a baking sheet and bake in a hot oven for 20 to 30 minutes or till the sesame seeds on top turn golden in colour.

Serving

Serve hot or cold along with green chutney or any sauce. This dish makes a good meal along with cheese cream or Russian salad.

Preparatory Time: 1 hour

Mushroom Health Bhel

Ingredients

Mushrooms (finely chopped)	1 cup	Lime juice	2 tbsp
Onion (finely chopped)	1 no.	Green chilli	3 nos
		Coriander (finely chopped)	½ cup
Tomato (finely chopped)	1 no.	Peanuts (soaked)	¼ cup
Cucumber (finely chopped)	1 no.	Imli (tamarind) chutney	2 tbsp
Moong sprouts/ fresh corn (boiled)	½ cup	Green chutney	1 tbsp

Optional for Gourmets

Aaloo/Bikaneri bhujia	¼ cup	Papries (crushed)	6 nos
Fried moong dal	¼ cup	Murmura (puffed rice)	1 cup

Preparation

1) Mix all the fresh items together in a big bowl.
2) Add chutneys and mix lightly. Don't add any additional salt.
3) Gourmets can add optional bhujia/fried dal/murmura.

Serving

Serve immediately.

Preparatory Time: 15 mins

Mushroom and Potato Chops

Ingredients

Potatoes (boiled and mashed)	4 nos	Paneer grated	¼ cup
		Pepper powder	1 tsp
Butter	1 tbsp	Mushroom stuffing (as used for Stuffed Mushrooms)	1 cup
Fresh breadcrumbs	2 slices		
Salt	A pinch		
Dry breadcrumbs	¼ cup	Oil for shallow frying	

Preparation

1) Mix mashed potatoes, salt, pepper, butter, paneer and fresh breadcrumbs together. Divide into 4–6 equal portions.

2) Divide the mushroom mixture also. Take one portion potato and flatten on your palm.
3) Place one portion stuffing and seal it. Roll in dry crumbs. In this way, finish all portions.

Cooking

1) Heat oil on a thick tava or a frying pan and shallow fry all chops in it.
2) Lift and serve hot with any chutney or tomato sauce or both.

Note

Ideal for rainy days or an evening snack. This chop can also be used as a burger patti.

Preparatory Time: 40 mins

Steamed Mushroom Nuggets

Ingredients

Mushrooms	200 gm	Ginger-garlic paste	2 tsp
Urad dal (dhuli)	4 tbsp	Baking soda	1 tsp
Moong dal (split)	2 tbsp	Mint powder	1 tsp
Semolina	3 tbsp	Salt	To taste
3 green chillies	4 nos		

For Tempering

Oil	2 tbsp	Asafoetida (hing powder)	½ tsp
Mustard seeds	1 tsp		
Curry leaves	2 sprigs	Coriander (chopped)	¼ cup

Preparation

1) Soak urad dal and moong dal together for 2 hours.

2) Chop mushrooms very finely just before using.

3) Drain dals. Grind together dals and green chillies. Add baking soda and mushrooms. Put salt and semolina, mix and keep aside for one hour.

4) Season cocktail idli moulds.

Cooking

1) Put 1½ cup water in a pressure cooker or idli steamer and let it boil.

2) Meanwhile, put 1 tsp batter in each depression of cocktail idli moulds and place in the steaming vessel.

3) Steam on full flame for 15-20 minutes.

4) Remove and cool the steamed nuggets. Remove with butter knife.

Tempering

Heat oil in pan and crackle mustard seeds. Add asafoetida, curry leaves, coriander and steamed nuggets. Mix well.

Serving

Serve hot with tomato sauce as a starter or an evening snack.

Preparatory Time: 20 mins

Mushroom and Vegetable Pie with Potato Topping

Ingredients

For Mushroom Stuffing

Mushroom (finely chopped)	1 cup	Yellow pepper (finely chopped)	1 no.
Spring onion (finely chopped with greens)	2 nos	Cauliflower (grated)	¼ cup
		Paneer (grated)	½ cup
Carrot (finely chopped)	1 no.	Mint (chopped)	2 tbsp
		Ginger and garlic	1 tsp each
Green pepper (finely chopped)	1 no.	Green chillies	2 nos
		Seasonings	To taste

For Pie

Potatoes (boiled)	4 nos	Milk	¼ cup
Butter	2 tbsp	Salt	A pinch

Preparation and Cooking

1) Peel and boil potatoes. Mash when still hot. Add butter, milk and salt. Mash well and keep aside.

2) Sauté onions and greens in butter. Add carrots and mushrooms and stir-fry.

3) Add cauliflower and cook for 1 minute. Add peppers and ginger and garlic paste. Fry for 2 minutes. Add seasonings and mix well.

4) Lastly add grated paneer and mix. Remove from fire. Add finely chopped green chillies and finely chopped mint.

5) Heat oven moderately.

6) Smear oil nicely in heat-proof flatter dish or a pie dish.

7) Put mushroom mixture in dish and spread well with a spatula evenly.

8) Now roll potatoes into a thick disk the size of the dish and cover pie with potato topping. Make design with fork and pinch outer rim with fingers.

9) Bake for 30 to 40 minutes.

Serving

Serve hot with any Continental meal. Enjoy it as it is with any clear soup.

Preparatory Time: 30 mins

Mushroom Dip

Ingredients

Mushrooms (chopped)	¾ cup	Milk	2 cups
		Salt	½ tsp
Butter	2 tbsp	Pepper	Few grains
Flour	2 tbsp	Mustard sauce	A pinch

Preparation and Cooking

1) Melt butter, blend in flour, gradually add milk.
2) Cook on slow fire, stirring constantly, until thick or cook on double boiler or on hot water till thick.
3) Add salt and pepper and stir constantly.

4) Add mushroom along with seasonings and cook for 5 minutes.

5) When cool, pass through liquidiser. Use when required. Store under refrigeration.

Serving

Ideal for serving with steamed vegetables or grilled chicken. Vegetable sticks and soup sticks can be served with this dip as starters in a cocktail party.

Preparatory Time: 20 mins

Gourmet Mushroom Balls

Ingredients

Mushrooms (finely chopped and slightly cooked)	1 cup	Garam masala	2 tbsp
		Eggs	2 nos
		Cooking oil	3 tbsp
Walnuts (broken)	1 cup	Tomato puree	1 cup
Garlic cloves	2 nos	White vinegar	1 tbsp
Carrot	1 no.	Water	3 cups
Celery (finely chopped)	1 tbsp	Onion (small) minced	1 no.
Coriander	2 tbsp	Capsicum minced	1 no.
Whole wheat/brown breadcrumbs	½ cup	Pepper powder	1 tsp
		Nutmeg	A pinch
Wheat flour and gram flour mixed	¼ cup + ¼ cup	Potli of garam masala (whole spices tied in a pouch)	

Preparation

1) Mix walnuts, mushrooms, garlic, onion, celery, carrot and coriander together and grind.

2) Add garam masala and dry breadcrumbs, gram flour and wheat flour mixed and eggs. Mix well.

3) Shape into lemon-sized balls. Sauté balls until browned on all sides in oil.

4) Combine together tomato puree, tomato sauce, water and potli of garam masala.

5) Boil and add balls and simmer for 1 hour.

Serving

Serve hot garnished with extra coriander. Serve with rice or dinner rolls or pavs.

Preparatory Time: 1½ hour

Mushroom in Hot Tomato Sauce with Rice/Noodles

Ingredients

Mushrooms (halved)	300 gm	Oil	3 tbsp
Onion (finely chopped)	1 large	Red chilli powder	1 tbsp
Tomatoes (pureed)	3 nos	Coriander (chopped)	3 tbsp
Garlic (finely chopped)	3 tbsp	Corn flour	1 tbsp
Ginger (finely chopped)	3 tbsp	Red chilli (whole)	2 nos
		Water	2 cups
		Salt	To taste/ optional

Cooking

1) Heat oil and add red chillies whole after removing seeds, so that the oil turns into chilli oil.

2) Sauté onions in hot oil, add garlic and stir-fry till golden. Add ginger and tomato puree. Fry till oil starts oozing out, now add chilli powder and 2 tbsp coriander, fry for a while.

3) Add halved mushrooms and fry for a minute or two.

4) Put water and boil for 5 minutes or till the gravy starts thickening.

5) Now mix corn flour with a little water and put into the gravy. Keep stirring so that no lump is formed. Boil for a minute and remove.

Serving

Serve hot garnished with rest of the coriander with rice, boiled noodles or parantha.

Serves 4 persons when the other dishes are also served.

Variation

Add 1 cup boiled green peas. Then you may use only 200 gm mushrooms.

Preparatory Time: 15 mins

Mushroom Koftas

Ingredients

For Koftas

Mushrooms	200 gm	Coriander (chopped)	2 tbsp
Chana dal	¼ cup		
Moong dal (split)	¼ cup	Peanuts	2–3 tbsp
Ginger	1-inch piece	Baking powder	1 tsp
		Salt	To taste
Green chillies	6 nos	Oil	For frying

For Curry

Onions	3 nos	Garam masala	1 tsp
Tomatoes	4 nos	Cumin seeds	1 tsp
Ginger-garlic paste	1 tbsp	Coriander (chopped)	3 tbsp
Turmeric powder	1 tsp	Water	6 cups
Red chilli powder	1½ tsp	Salt	To taste

Preparation

1) Soak dals for 2 hours minimum and grind.
2) As you grind add green chillies, ginger, coriander.
3) Grate mushrooms.
4) Remove dal batter and add grated mushrooms and baking soda. Keep aside for one hour.
5) Chop onions and tomatoes for gravy.
6) Powder peanuts.
7) Add salt and peanut powder to the dal and mushroom mixture. Mix well.

Cooking

1) Heat oil.
2) With a teaspoon keep dropping the batter in hot oil, fry and remove on kitchen paper. Finish all the mixture this way.
3) In the same oil fry the chopped onions to golden brown colour, remove and keep aside.
4) In a grinder put chopped tomatoes and onions. Grind to a paste.
5) Heat 4 tbsp oil in another pan and crackle cumin in it.
6) Put onion and tomato paste in it and fry till it starts leaving oil.
7) Add ginger-garlic paste, turmeric, chilli and garam masala powders and cook for 2 minutes. If the paste starts sticking to the pan, sprinkle a little water on it. Add 2 tbsp chopped coriander, water and salt in it.

8) Bring the gravy to boiling point and simmer for 30 minutes or pressure-cook for 10 minutes and then simmer for 5 minutes. The gravy should be thin.

9) Add koftas in hot gravy 15 minutes before serving.

Serving

Garnish kofta curry with saved coriander leaves and serve hot with steamed rice or hot chapatti.

Note

If you like these koftas without gravy, use as starters.

Preparatory Time: 45 mins

Vegetarian Stock

Preparation

1) Roughly chop 1 carrot, 1 onion, 3–4 leaves cabbage, stems of spinach/coriander etc., 10 peppercorns, 2 black cardamoms, 1 bay leaf, ½-inch stick of cinnamon, 1 large tomato.

2) Mix everything together and add 6 cups water and boil.

3) Boil for 10 minutes on full flame and then simmer for 30–40 minutes.

4) Roughly mash vegetables with eggbeater or a wooden spoon and then drain and keep aside.

5) Ideal to be used with any gravy or soup.

Note

Stock can be prepared in advance and kept under refrigeration till used for soups and gravies.

Preparatory Time: 1 hour

Fried Chicken with Brown Mushroom Sauce

Ingredients

For Mushroom Sauce

Mushrooms halved	300 gm	Bay leaf	1 no.
Onions chopped finely	2 nos	Basil powder/ fresh basil	1 tsp/1 tbsp
Ginger grated	2 tbsp	Grated cheese	¼ cup
Butter	3 tbsp	Corn flour	2 tbsp
Veg/non-veg stock	2½ cups	Salt to taste	
Pepper powder	2 tsp		

For Fried Chicken

Chicken	1 no.	Salt	1 tsp
Vinegar	¼ cup	Eggs	2 nos
Pepper powder	1 tsp	Breadcrumbs	1 cup
Soya sauce	1 tsp	Oil for frying	
Chilli sauce	1 tsp		

Preparation

1) Clean, wash and cut chicken into 8 pieces.

2) Mix vinegar, salt, pepper, soya and chilli sauce. Marinate chicken pieces with this marinade and stand for 1 hour minimum.

3) Add 1 cup water to the marinated chicken and cook chicken covered with a lid till the water dries up. Open the lid and cool the contents.

4) Beat eggs with a pinch of salt and keep aside.

5) Heat oil in a frying pan.

Cooking

1) Dip chicken pieces in beaten egg and roll in breadcrumbs, deep fry till golden in colour. Place them on kitchen paper and keep aside.

2) Now heat butter in a separate pan and sauté chopped onions. And ginger and corn flour. Fry till brown in colour.

3) Add stock salt, pepper and bay leaf. Bring to boiling point and then lower heat. Cook the sauce stirring constantly to avoid any lumps till it thickens a bit.

4) Add mushrooms and basil and cook for 5 minutes.

5) Add soya sauce and remove.

6) Add ¼ cup cream if you desire creamer sauce. Cover and keep aside.

Assembly

Arrange the fried chicken pieces in a shallow oven-proof dish and pour the mushroom sauce over. Sprinkle grated cheese and heat in an oven for 10 to 15 minutes before serving.

Preparatory Time: 45 mins

Non-vegetarian Stock

Preparation

For non-veg stock add chicken or mutton bones (soup bones) to the previously mentioned ingredients (in Vegetarian Stock) and cook for 1 hour.

Note

Stock can be prepared in advance and kept under refrigeration till used for soups and gravies.

Preparatory Time: 1 hour

Mushroom and Chicken Pie with Crisp Pastry

Ingredients

For Plain One-crust Pastry

Flour	1½ cup	Butter	½ cup
Salt	½ tsp	Water	3 tbsp chilled

For Stuffing

Mushrooms (sliced)	1 cup	Cream	½ cup
Green peas (boiled)	¼ cup	Egg yolk	1 no.
Capsicum (chopped)	¼ cup	Butter	2 tbsp
Chicken (boiled/cooked/diced)	1½ cup	Red pepper (chopped)	2 tbsp
White sauce	1½ cup	Basil powder	½ tsp
		Salt and pepper	To taste

Preparation for Pastry

1) Sieve flour and salt together. Add butter to flour and mix it with your fingertips till the flour resembles breadcrumbs.

2) Now add cold water to hold the ingredients together. Sprinkle a little more cold water evenly and form a ball.

3) Roll out dough in circular shape on lightly floured board.

4) Pie should be about 1/8-inch thick. Fit into 8-inch or 9-inch pie shell. Trim pastry to 1-inch of edge of pie pan/shell, fold underneath.

5) Pinch pastry edges or press with fork. Prick the bottom with fork too.

6) Bake it blind in very hot oven for 15 mins (450 degrees F). Keep aside.

Preparation for Stuffing

1) Brown mushrooms and capsicums in butter.

2) Mix cream, green peas, white sauce, chicken, salt, pepper etc.

3) Heat over hot water. Beat egg yolk and add to the chicken mixture.

4) Heat stirring constantly for 1 minute.

Serving

Serve in the baked pie shell.

Preparatory Time: 40 mins

Mushroom Relish (Raita)

Ingredients

Mushrooms	200 gm	Green chillies chopped	2 nos
Curds	2 cups	Pepper	2 tsp
Gelatine	2 tbsp	Butter	1 tbsp
Ginger grated	1 tbsp	Salt	To taste
Fresh basil chopped	2 tbsp	Small ice-cream cups	4 nos

Preparation and Cooking

1) Clean and place ice-cream cups under refrigeration.
2) Chop mushrooms.
3) Dissolve gelatine in 6 tbsp water on a pan of hot water.

4) Heat butter and sauté mushrooms in it. Remove and cool.

5) Mix together curds, ginger, chillies, basil, salt and pepper. Beat lightly and mix gelatine in it. Cool on the pan of ice. Keep stirring to avoid any lumps.

6) Put cooked mushrooms in an electric blender and churn for a while. Add mushroom mixture to the prepared curds. Keep stirring and let it thicken.

7) Pour mixture in 4 ice-cream cups and place in a refrigerator till use.

Serving

Garnish each cup with 1 leaf of basil and serve the dish cold.

This relish makes an excellent accompaniment to any Indian or Continental meal.

Variation

Instead of basil you may use fresh mint leaves for flavour.

Note

All ingredients used in this dish must be at room temperature.

Preparatory Time: 30 mins

Mushroom Jodhpuri

Ingredients

Mushrooms	400 gm	Ajwain	1 tsp
Tomato puree	2 cups	Basil	1 tsp
Chilli garlic	½ cup	Cream	¼ cup (optional)
Butter	4 tbsp	Salt to taste	

Preparation

Wash and cut mushrooms into halves.

Cooking

1) Heat butter, add ajwain and crackle.
2) Put tomato puree in it and cook for 5 minutes.
3) Add chilli garlic and cook till fat oozes.

4) Add salt and mushrooms, cook for 5 minutes. Add basil and cover for another 5 minutes and reduce heat.

5) Remove and check salt. Add cream and serve hot with any chapatti, pav or boiled rice.

Note

This preparation is chilli hot. If you don't like much chillies, reduce the quantity of chilli garlic sauce.

Variation

Along with mushrooms use other mixed vegetables like carrots and cauliflower. You may use only paneer pieces in the same gravy.

Preparatory Time: 20 mins

Mushroom Soup (Bisque)

Ingredients

Mushrooms	2 cups sliced	Egg yolk	1 no. (optional)
Water/chicken stock	4 cups	Fresh cream	4 tbsp
Onion	1 no. sliced	Coriander chopped	¼ cup finely
Garlic	2 cloves	Pepper	2 tsp
Butter	2 tbsp	Tabasco sauce	A few drops
Flour	2 tbsp	Salt	To taste
Milk	2 cups		

Cooking

1) Put 1½ cup mushroom slices, water/stock, onions and garlic together in a vessel and cook for 30 minutes.
2) Cool and pass through a liquidiser.
3) Heat butter and add flour, stir till it is pinkish, switch off the flame and add milk slowly. Cook on slow fire for 10 minutes.
4) Add mushroom puree and cook for another 5–10 minutes. It should make 4-6 servings. If required, add a little water or milk.
5) Beat egg yolk and mix with the mushroom mixture.
6) Check for seasonings. Add ½ cup saved mushrooms and coriander.

Serving

Whip cream and add one tsp in each soup bowl. Pour hot soup and serve with crusty bread/soup sticks or even crispy khakra. With one good salad it makes a complete meal.

Note

Bisque: A heavy cream soup of pureed meats and vegetables.

Khakra: A very thin and crisp chapatti, favourite of Gujaratis in India. Now available commercially in leading stores all over India.

Preparatory Time: 45 mins

Buttered Mushroom

Ingredients

Mushrooms	400 gm	Pepper powder	1 cup
Butter	3 to 4 tbsp	Soya Sauce	2 tbsp
Coriander (chopped)	1 cup	Salt to taste (optional)	
		Toothpicks	

Preparation

Remove the stems of mushrooms and cut into halves.

Cooking

1) Heat butter thoroughly and add chopped coriander leaves and fry for one minute.

2) Add mushrooms, salt, pepper and soya sauce. Fry till all the liquid is dried and the preparation is nice and shining.

Serving

Place buttered mushrooms in a flat dish and served hot along with toothpicks as starters.

Variation

You may serve the prepared mushrooms in a sizzler dish. For that heat the sizzling dish till very hot, spread cabbage leaves and put some butter under the leaves. Quickly arrange buttered mushrooms and serve sizzling hot.

Preparatory Time: 10 mins

Mushroom Goulash

Ingredients

Mushrooms	200 gm	Vinegar	¼ cup
Mutton (boneless)	200 gm	Pepper corns	12 nos
Madras onions	12 nos	Black cardamoms	3 nos
or		Cinnamon powder	½ tsp
Spring onions with greens	6 nos	Pepper powder	1 tsp
		Butter	2 tbsp
Green pepper	1 no.	Water	6 cups
Red pepper	1 no.	Salt	To taste
Tomatoes	2 large (skinned)	Coriander	¼ cup chopped for garnish
Ginger-garlic paste	1 tbsp		
Corn flour	2–3 tbsp		

Preparation

1) Cut boneless meat into half-inch pieces. Sprinkle 1 tsp salt and pepper powder. Add vinegar and mix. Marinate for 1–2 hours or keep for more time under refrigeration.

2) Cut mushrooms into halves.

3) Cut red and green peppers into half-inch pieces.

4) Skin tomatoes and cut into half-inch quarters.

5) Chop greens of spring onions and clean spring onions or madras onions but keep them whole.

Cooking

1) Heat butter in a pressure cooker and add whole spices. Crackle.

2) Add onions without green and fry till pinkish.

3) Add marinated meat and ginger-garlic paste. Fry for 2–3 minutes on high flame.

4) Add corn flour and brown it.

5) Add 2 cups water and pressure-cook for 15 minutes or till meat pieces are tender.

6) Add rest of the vegetables, mushrooms and 4 cups water. Bring to boiling point and then simmer for 35–40 minutes. Remove. Check for seasonings.

Serving

Garnish with chopped coriander and serve the stew hot with crisp bread or toasts.

Note

For a light dish this is a complete meal. If you like the dish chilli hot, use Tabasco or Capsico sauce. A few drops can enhance the flavour.

Goulash: A stew of meat, vegetables and seasonings.

Preparatory Time: 1 hour

Mushroom and Spinach Salad

Ingredients

Mushrooms sliced	2 cups	Spring onions chopped	½ cup
Fresh spinach chopped	2 cups	Cucumber cubed	1 no.
Soaked peanuts	½ cup	Grated fresh coconut	¼ cup
Kidney beans boiled	½ cup	Honey Lemon Dressing	½ cup

Preparation

For Honey Lemon Dressing
Mix Together

Table vinegar	¼ cup	Cooking oil	1 tsp
Fresh lemon juice	2 tbsp	Pepper powder	2 tsp
Honey	2 tbsp	Salt to taste (optional)	

Combine these ingredients and chill before use.

Assembly

Take a platter and spread chopped spinach. Mixed all the other ingredients and pour dressing over them. Arrange them carefully on the spinach bed.

Serving

Serve this salad cold along with any meal.

Preparatory Time: 15 mins

Mushroom and Vegetable Stew

Ingredients

Mushroom	200 gm halved/ quartered	Onion	1 large cut into 1-inch pieces
Carrots	½ cup boiled	Garlic	1 tbsp chopped
Cauliflower	½ cup cut into small pieces	Peppercorns	10–12 nos
		Black cardamom	3 nos
Capsicums (green)	2 nos cut into ½-inch pieces	Potato	1 large (optional)
		Cinnamon	1-inch stick
Tomatoes	2 nos skinned and chopped	Corn flour/flour	2 tbsp
		Butter	2 tbsp
Ginger	1-inch piece grated	Coriander/parsley	1 tbsp
		Water	5 cups

Cooking

1) Heat butter and sauté onions, add garlic and fry. Add spices.

2) Add cauliflower, carrots and ginger. Stir-fry for 1 minute.

3) Add corn flour and mix nicely till it turns brownish.

4) Add water and salt. Let vegetables cook till tender.

5) Now add capsicums and tomatoes, boil for 2-3 minutes.

6) Add quartered mushrooms and boil for another 3 minutes.

7) Check seasonings.

8) Finally add chopped coriander or parsley. Remove.

Serving

Serve hot with plain toasted and buttered bread or garlic bread or even dinner rolls.

Note

If the stew is thin in consistency, add a little more corn flour mixed with 2 tbsp water.

Preparatory Time: 30 mins

Mushroom Savoury Omelette

Ingredients

Mushrooms chopped finely	200 gm	Milk	8 tbsp
Spring onions chopped	4 nos	Pepper powder	2 tsp
Green chillies chopped	6 nos	Butter	2 tbsp
Tomatoes skinned and chopped	2 nos	Eggs	8 nos.
		Cheese grated (optional)	¼ cup
Coriander chopped	½ cup	Salt to taste (optional)	
		Oil for making omelettes	

Preparation

1) Beat 2 eggs at a time with 2 tbsp milk, a pinch of salt and pepper each.

2) Heat butter and add chopped spring onions with greens, mushrooms, tomatoes, 1 tsp salt and pepper each. Cook on high flame stirring constantly till vegetables are almost dry, add coriander and green chillies. Remove and cool.

Making Omelettes

1) Take a heavy bottomed non-stick pan, heat it and grease with 1 tsp oil. Lower the heat.

2) Put 2 beaten eggs in it and tilt the pan to spread the eggs. With a wooden spatula stir the eggs from the centre.

3) When eggs are half set, place 2 to 3 tbsp mushroom stuffing in the centre of the eggs lengthwise and sprinkle a little grated cheese over it.

4) Fold omelette from both sides and gently turn its side with the spatula. Drop a little oil on sides, if required. Cook till golden brown and serve hot. To make it chilli hot, add a few drops of Capsico or Tabasco over it.

Serving

Serve hot omelette with crisp buttered toasts and tomato sauce. To wash it down add hot or cold coffee, hot tea or any flavoured milk to your breakfast or brunch.

Note

This dish is ideal for growing children and egg-lovers. It makes the Sunday breakfast special.

Preparatory Time: 15 mins

Mushroom Loaf

Ingredients

Mushrooms	2 cups (finely chopped)	Breadcrumbs (brown)	1 cup
Onion	¼ cup (finely chopped)	Potatoes (boiled and mashed)	1 cup
Green peppers	One-third cup (chopped)	Cheese (grated)	½ cup
		Sesame seeds (roasted and powdered)	½ cup
		Crushed walnuts	½ cup
Tomatoes (chopped)	½ cup	Ginger (grated)	2-inch piece
or		Chilli-garlic sauce	1 tbsp
		Dried mint powder	2 tbsp
Tomato puree	¼ cup	Eggs	2 nos

Preparation

1) Mix all the ingredients together.
2) Grease a loaf tin.
3) Sprinkle with a little breadcrumbs and press together in the loaf tin.

Baking

Bake in a moderately hot oven for 30–40 minutes or till done. It should be slightly firm. Remove and cool. Cover the mould with a foil and put it under refrigeration for 5 to 6 hours before use. Invert and cut into slices.

Serving

Serve it with any Continental meal.

Note

If using a cooking range, keep some water in a pan on the lower shelf, so that the loaf does not become too dry.

Preparatory Time: 45 mins

Mushroom Panchratan

Ingredients

Mushrooms	200 gm	Garam masala	1 tsp
Green chutney	1 cup	Green chilli paste	1 tsp
Almonds	25 nos	Cumin	1 tsp
Onions fried	½ cup	Paneer cubes	½ cup
Curds	¼ cup	Green peas	½ cup
Cream	¼ cup	Raisins/fresh grapes	¼ cup
Spinach puree	¼ cup	Almonds	20 nos
Butter	3 tbsp	Salt	To taste

Tempering

Oil	1 tsp
Red chillies whole	2 nos
Mustard seeds	½ tsp

Preparation

1) Grind fried onions with ½ cup water and keep aside.
2) Soak 25 almonds for 1 hour and boil for 5 minutes or microwave for 2 minutes and grind ¼ cup curd.
3) Boil green peas.
4) Wash and cut mushrooms into halves.
5) Soak raisins in half cup water.

Cooking

1) Heat 1 tsp oil and fry 20 almonds in it and remove.
2) Add butter to the same oil and crackle cumin in it.
3) Add onion paste and green chutney. Fry nicely.
4) Add almond paste and stir-fry for a few seconds.
5) Add green chilli paste and garam masala. Add 2 cups water, boil and then simmer for 10–15 minutes.
6) Add spinach puree and cream together. Add salt according to the paste.
7) Add mushrooms, peas, raisins, almonds and paneer cubes. Cook for 5 minutes or till the gravy is nice and smooth. Remove from fire and pour in a serving bowl.
8) For tempering, heat oil, crackle mustard seeds in it and add red chillies. Pour tempering over the prepared dish just before serving.

Serving

Serve hot with naan, parantha or hot chapattis.

Variation

- You may just add 400 gm mushrooms in this gravy and omit peas, paneer, almonds and raisins.
- You may add any other four vegetables along with mushrooms in the same gravy.

Preparatory Time: 35 mins

Chilli Garlic Sauce

Ingredients

Dry red chillies	100 gm	Vinegar	½ cup
Garlic (peeled)	1 cup	Oil	¼ cup
Salt	3 tsp		

Preparation

1) Remove the seeds of chillies and break the stems. Soak in 2 cups water for 1 hour and cook chillies in the same water. Boil, then cover and simmer till about 1 cup water is left. Remove from heat and cool.

2) Put chillies, garlic, vinegar and salt in a blender and blend till smooth.

3) Heat oil to smoking point and turn off heat. Now add the chilli mixture to it. Cool for some time and store under refrigeration. Use as and when required.

Preparatory Time: 30 mins

Mushroom Stuffed Potli Chicken

Ingredients

Chicken	1 no.	Garlic paste	1 ts
Lemon juice	3 tbsp	Chilli sauce	1 ts
Pepper powder	1 tsp	Salt	2 ts
Ginger paste	1 tsp	Oil	1 ts

Clean chicken and dry it with the kitchen towe
Mix together lemon juice, salt, pepper, ginger-garli
paste and chilli sauce. Apply this mixture to the chicke
nicely. Smear the inside of the chicken too. Keep aside

For Stuffing

Mushrooms   200 gm

| Spring onions with greens | 2 nos |
| Carrot | 1 no. |

Slice everything and stuff the chicken with these ingredients.

For the Shell

Salt	1 kg
Wheat flour	½ kg
Foil for wrapping chicken	

Preparation

1) Heat baking oven to moderate heat.
2) Wrap stuffed chicken in aluminium foil properly covering all sides.
3) Mix together salt and wheat flour. Using water, make a smooth dough. Knead properly so that dough is pliable and not hard. Roll dough into a large, thick chapatti.
4) Keep wrapped chicken in the centre of the rolled chapatti and cover it properly over the foil so that juices of the chicken do not run out.
5) Bake wrapped chicken in hot oven for 2 hours or till the chicken shell is hard and brown. Remove from oven and keep aside.

Serving

Break the hard shell with a hammer and remove the wrapped chicken from it. Open the foil and serve hot chicken on the bed of lettuce leaves. If some liquid from the vegetables flows down, collect and pour it over the chicken. The stuffed vegetables impart a nice taste.

Note

This is a high protein and low calorie health dish so anyone can consume it. If you desire it hot, mushroom sauce can be served with the preparation.

Preparatory Time: 3 hours

Mushroom Jhinga Biryani

Ingredients

Mushrooms	400 gm	Cinnamon	2 cloves
Prawns	250 gm	Cumin	1 tsp
Rice	2 cups	Oil	4 tbsp
Onions fried	1 cup	Water	3 cups
Tomato puree	1 cup	Milk	1 cup
Ginger-garlic paste	2 tbsp	Saffron	10 strands
Turmeric powder	1 tsp	Coriander and mint chopped	½ cup
Chilli powder	2 tsp		
Garam masala	1 tbsp	Green chillies chopped	4 nos
Pepper corn	12 nos.		
Green cardamom	6 nos.	Lime juice	4 tbsp
Bay leaf	2 nos.	Oil	3 tbsp
		Chapatti dough to seal the vessel	

Preparation

1) Take ½ cup fried onions and ½ cup water.
2) Mix and pass through liquidiser.
3) Par boil rice in enough water along with pepper corns, cardamoms, bay leaves, cinnamon and 1 tsp salt. Drain and keep aside.
4) Luke warm the milk and add saffron to it.

Cooking

1) Heat 4 tbsp oil and add 1 tsp cumin seeds. Crackle. Add onion paste, ginger-garlic paste, turmeric and chilli powder and tomato puree. Fry for 2–3 minutes and add garam masala and 3 cups water. Boil and simmer for 5 minutes. Add mushrooms and prawns. Cook for another 5 minutes and check the salt.
2) Take a heavy bottomed pan/vessel with a lid and heat it. Put 2 tbsp oil in it and spread evenly on bottom of the pan. Lower the heat. Sprinkle some boiled rice on it and cover the bottom. Place half the mushroom and prawn masala over it evenly. Sprinkle a handful of coriander and mint, a few green chillies and half of the fried onions. Sprinkle half of the lemon juice also. Repeat the process till all the rice is finished. End with the rice. Sprinkle a little coriander and mint on top. With a knife make a few depressions and sprinkle saffron and milk mixture. Pour the rest of the lemon juice evenly over the rice.
3) Place the lid and seal it properly with the chapatti dough.
4) Place a tava (iron plate) on the fire and put this vessel on it. Cook on medium fire for 45–60 minutes. Break the seal just before serving.

Serving

Take a rice plate and spread cooked biryani in it carefully. Garnish with a few mint leaves and serve hot with plain curd or any raita.

Tip

You can prepare mushroom and prawn mixture in advance and boil the rice too. Place under refrigeration and assemble 2 hours before consumption.

Preparatory Time: 1 hour 15 mins

Mushroom Sauce

Ingredients

Mushrooms	1 cup	Pepper powder	1 tsp
Milk	1½ cup	Mustard powder	½ tsp
Butter	2 tbsp	Bay leaf	1 no.
Flour	1 tbsp	Chopped parsley/basil	1 tbsp

Preparation

1) Wash and chop mushrooms and stalks finely.

2) Heat butter and add flour. Stir over low heat till the flour is just pink. Turn off heat and now gently add milk in a small quantity. Keep stirring briskly till the sauce is smooth.

3) Turn on heat and add mushrooms and bay leaf. Simmer for 10 minutes or till the lovely aroma of cooked flour starts spreading around you.

4) Remove from fire and lift out the bay leaf.

5) Add pepper and mustard powder in it. Sprinkle with parsley or basil.

Serving

Use with any bread or pasta.

Preparatory Time: 20 mins

Chicken Mushroom Delight

Ingredients

Chicken mince	200 gm	Pepper powder	1 tsp
Mushrooms	100 gm	Dry yeast	2 tsp
Spring onions	2 nos	Milk	2 tbsp
Capsicums	1 no.	Sugar	½ tsp
Ginger powder	1 tsp	Oil	For frying
Chilli-garlic sauce	1 tsp	Salt	To taste

Preparation

1) Chop spring onions and capsicums.
2) Take lukewarm milk, add sugar and yeast. Mix and keep aside for 10–15 minutes. Use when it starts bubbling.

3) Put chicken mince in an electric blender. Add chopped onion, capsicum, pepper and ginger powder. Add salt too. Grind to a fine paste.

4) Add bubbling yeast too. Mix once again and keep aside for 2 hours.

Cooking

1) Heat oil.
2) Wet your hands with water and make small balls.
3) Fry them on medium fire.

Serving

Serve hot with green chutney.

Preparatory Time: 15 mins

Cream of Mushroom and Celery Soup

Ingredients

Mushrooms	1 cup very finely chopped	Butter	1 tbsp
		Corn flour	1 tbsp
Celery	1 stick chopped	Milk and water	1 cup
Pepper	1 tsp levelled	Salt	To taste (optional)
Veg/Non-veg stock	5 cups		

Cooking

1) Place mushrooms and celery in pan and boil for 10 minutes.

2) In another pan heat butter and add corn flour, fry for a few seconds or till it is pink.

3) Add milk and water, bring to boil.

4) Simmer for 2 mins.; mix mushroom and celery soup.

5) Add salt and pepper. Simmer for 5 minutes.

Serving

Serve hot garnished with cream. Soup sticks, toasted bread slices or buttered dinner rolls are ideal accompaniments.

Variation

You may add finely chopped carrots, capsicums, cauliflower or even finely shredded chicken pieces. You may garnish it with chopped coriander.

Preparatory Time: 25 mins

Stir-fried Mushroom with Spinach

Ingredients

Washed and chopped spinach	3 cups (1 bundle)	Garlic sliced	1 tbsp
Halved/sliced mushrooms	2 cups	Chilli-garlic	1 tsp
		Red chillies (whole)	2 nos
Onion sliced	1 no.	Soya sauce	1 tsp
		Oil	2 tbsp

Cooking

1) Heat oil and add red chillies. Add onion and stir till golden.
2) Add chopped garlic and stir-fry till pink.

3) Add chilli-garlic and spinach. Stir-fry for 2–3 minutes.
4) Add chopped mushrooms and keep stirring till the water dries up and the vegetables are nice and shining.
5) Add soya sauce and mix well.
6) Remove from the fire and serve hot.

Note

No salt has been added to this dish because spinach, mushroom and soya sauce have enough natural salts.

Preparatory Time: 10 mins

Mushroom Pizza

Ingredients

Pizza shells	4 nos	Olives halved	12 nos
Mushrooms sliced	2 cups	Mozzarella cheese grated	1½ cup
Capsicums thinly sliced	2 nos	Pizza sauce	1½ cup

For Pizza Sauce

Onions chopped finely	2 nos	Oregano	2 tsp
Tomato puree	2 cups	Clove powder	1 tsp
Butter	3 tbsp	Sugar	1 tbsp
Ajwain	1 tsp	Pepper	2 tsp
Chilli-garlic paste	1 tbsp	Finely cubed capsicum	¼ cup
Red chilli powder	1 tsp	Salt to taste	

Preparation and Cooking

1) Heat butter, add ajwain and crackle.
2) Put chopped onions and fry till light brown.
3) Add ginger-garlic paste and tomato puree. Fry for 5 minutes.
4) Add red chilli powder, clove powder, salt, sugar, pepper and capsicums. Fry for 2 minutes.
5) Finally add oregano and check seasonings. Remove from fire and cool.

Assembly

1) Pre-heat oven.
2) Take 1 pizza shell and smear nicely with pizza sauce.
3) Sprinkle a little cheese and arrange chopped mushrooms, 6 pieces of olives and sliced capsicums. Top it with grated cheese.
4) Cover from all sides and place in hot oven for 8–10 minutes or till cheese melts.

Serving

Cut the prepared pizza into 6 wedges and serve hot with mustard sauce.

Variation

Along with mushrooms, you can top pizzas with baby corns, pineapple slices, tomato wedges and any kind of chicken meat.

Preparatory Time: 30 mins

Pasta in Mushroom Sauce

Ingredients

Pasta	200 gm	Chilli-garlic	1 tsp
Mushrooms washed and sliced	200 gm	Coriander chopped	1 tbsp
Cheese	30 gm	Ginger	1-inch piece
Butter	2 tbsp		
Tomatoes	4 nos	Corn flour	1 tbsp
Onion finely chopped	1 large	Salt and pepper	To taste

Cooking

1) Boil pasta with 1 tsp salt and 1 tsp oil in enough water. When cooked drain the water and rinse pasta in cold water. Keep aside.

2) Heat butter, brown onion to golden stage.

3) Pass tomatoes through electric blender, strain and mix with fried onions and fry further.

4) Grate ginger root and add chilli-garlic. Fry for some time.

5) Add 2 cups water and boil for 5 minutes. Meanwhile, mix corn flour with a little water and put into the boiling sauce.

6) Add chopped mushrooms and coriander, boil for another 5 minutes on medium fire and remove.

7) Grate cheese.

Serving

Arrange boiled pasta in an ovenproof dish. Pour sauce over it and sprinkle grated cheese. Bake in hot oven for 15 minutes and serve hot.

Note

With any light soup and a salad this dish is a complete meal.

Preparatory Time: 40 mins

Spinach Pancakes in Cheese and Mushroom Sauce

Ingredients

For Pancakes (8 nos)

Flour	½ cup	Salt	A pinch
Milk	½ cup	Spinach puree	¼ cup
Egg	1 no.	Oil	1 tsp

For Cheese and Mushroom Sauce

Mushrooms (washed and sliced)	200 gm	Milk	3 cups
		Salt	A pinch
Flour	3 tbsp	Black/white pepper	1½ tsp
Butter	3 tbsp	Mustard powder	½ tsp

Onion	1 small	Bay leaf	1 no.
Cloves	3 nos	Cheese (grated)	50 gm/6 tbsp
		Ginger	1-inch piece

Preparation for Pancakes

1) Mix together flour, milk, egg and salt. Beat with beater till well mixed.

2) Mix spinach puree and oil, keep aside at least for half an hour.

3) Make pancakes on non-stick pan with one ladle of batter each. Finish and keep them warm.

Preparation for Mushroom Sauce

1) Heat butter and add flour, stir till it is just pinkish. Turn off heat.

2) Take lukewarm milk and add to the flour slowly and keep stirring to avoid lumps in the sauce.

3) Stick cloves to the peeled onion and drop it into the sauce. Add bay leaf. Return it to fire and cook on slow fire for 15–20 minutes or till the nice aroma of cooked flour wafts around. Turn off heat and remove onion and bay leaf.

4) Now add sliced mushrooms and cook for 5 mins. Remove from fire.

5) Mix 4 tbsp grated cheese, salt, pepper and mustard powder with the cooked sauce.

Assembly

1) Heat the oven.

2) Take an oven-proof dish and smear with oil from inside. Now cover the bottom completely with the pancake(s) green side up.

3) Spread a layer of sauce. Then just repeat the process of spreading pancakes and sauce till it is finished.

4) Sprinkle the rest of the grated cheese on top and bake in hot oven for half an hour or till the top is just golden pink.

Serving

Serve hot with garlic bread/dinner rolls.

Note

This is a very nutritious dish for growing children. For grown-ups it's a meal in itself. Just have soup and salad with this dish and no bread.

Preparatory Time: 1 hour

Mushroom Stuffed Baked Chicken Rolls

Ingredients

Chicken breasts	2 nos	Green chilli paste	1 tsp
Lime juice	4 tbsp	Salt	1 tsp
Ginger-garlic paste	1 tbsp		

Preparation

Make 4 to 6 fillets out of chicken meat. Mix ginger, garlic and chilli paste with salt and lime juice and rub on the chicken fillets. Keep aside for 4 hours. You may keep under refrigeration overnight. Take out and beat with the meat flattener. Keep aside.

Ingredients for Stuffing

Mushrooms chopped finely	150 gm
Onion chopped finely	¼ cup
Coriander chopped	¼ cup
Chilli sauce	1 tbsp
Fresh breadcrumbs	From 2 slices
MSG (Ajinomoto)	¼ tsp levelled
Salt	Optional
Oil	1 tbsp
Mushroom dip to serve with	2 cups
Foil cut into 6 pieces (9"×12")	

Cooking

1) Heat oil and sauté onions, add mushrooms and cook till almost dry. Add rest of the stuffing ingredients and mix properly over the fire. The filling should be dry. Divide into equal portions as per the number of fillets.

2) Heat oven for moderate heat.

3) Keep a baking tray ready.

4) Place one flattened chicken fillet on the chopping board and spread one portion of stuffing on it evenly. Now roll it properly and place on the piece of foil; roll foil over it covering the sides too. In this way, stuff all the fillets and roll in foil individually.

5) Place rolled fillets in baking tray on the upper shelf of the oven and bake for 40 to 45 minutes. Place a bowl of water too on the lower shelf.

6) Remove and cool the rolls under refrigeration. Remove the wrapped foil carefully and slice the rolls.

Serving

Arrange sliced chicken in a flatter dish and cover with the mushroom dip. You may enjoy the dish cold with cold meals in summers.

If you prefer it hot, place the dish in a traditional oven or in a microwave. This dish can be part of any Continental menu.

Note

You can enjoy sliced chicken rolls even without mushroom dip as a snack with mustard sauce or fresh coriander relish, or use them for making sandwiches.

Tip

The mushroom stuffed chicken rolls can be prepared in advance and kept in the deep freezer. Remove them 2 hours before use. Even the mushroom dip can be stored under refrigeration in a chill tray.

Preparatory Time: 1 hour

Batter Fried
Stuffed Mushroom

Ingredients

For Batter

Gram flour	1 cup levelled	Ginger-garlic paste	1 tsp
Corn flour	2 tbsp	Chilli powder	1 tsp levelled
Rice flour	2 tbsp	Kasoori methi	1 tsp
Baking powder	½ tsp	Salt to taste	
		Oil for frying	

Mix all the ingredients and make batter of dropping consistency using water. Let it stand for 30 minutes minimum and then use.

For Stuffing

Big mushrooms	16 nos	Oil	2 tbsp
Pumpkin grated	200 gm	Mango powder	1 tsp
Coriander chopped	½ cup	Garam masala	1 tsp
Green chillies chopped	4 nos	Salt to taste	
Paneer grated	½ cup		

Preparation and Cooking

1) Remove mushroom stems carefully and with the tip of a peeler clean the cavity properly.

2) Heat oil and add grated pumpkin, coriander, chilli, paneer, mango powder, garam masala and salt. Sauté.

3) Mash mushroom stems and add to the stuffing mixture. Mix well and cook on high flame. Cool the stuffing.

4) Stuff mushroom caps with the stuffing and if the stuffing is extra, spread on the mushrooms.

5) Heat oil properly and reduce heat to medium.

6) Beat the gram flour batter once again.

7) Dip the stuffed mushrooms one by one in the batter and fry 3 to 4 mushrooms at a time till crisp on all sides. Drain on kitchen paper. In this way, fry all the stuffed mushrooms.

Serving

Serve hot with Pumpkin Peels and Seeds Relish (chutney).

Pumpkin Peels and Seeds Chutney

Peels and seeds of pumpkin used for stuffing mushrooms.

Peanuts	1 tbsp	Oil	1 tbsp
Urad dal	1 tbsp	Curds	½ cup
Green chillies	2 nos	Salt	To taste

Cooking

1) Heat oil and fry urad dal and peanuts till golden.
2) Add pumpkin peels and seeds along with salt and cook for 5 minutes.
3) Cool and grind in an electric grinder.
4) Add curds and churn to dilute. Check the salt and temper it. Take out in a serving bowl.

Tempering

Heat 1 tsp oil, add a pinch of asafoetida and ¼ tsp mustard seeds, crackle and pour over chutney.

Tip

Stuffing for mushrooms and the relish of the peels and seeds can be made in advance and kept under refrigeration.

Preparatory Time: 45 mins

Mushroom Stuffed Moong Pancakes

Ingredients

For Pancakes

Moong dal (split/dhuli)	1 cup	Garlic (chopped)	1 tbsp
Urad dal (split/dhuli)	½ cup	Green chillies (chopped)	4–6 nos
Egg (beaten)	1 no.	Baking soda	1 tsp
Ginger (chopped)	1-inch piece	Salt	½ tsp
		Oil as much as required	

Preparation

1) Soak dals for 6 hours. If split dals are used, wash and slowly remove all green and black husk.

2) Pass dals with ½ cup water through liquidiser. While grinding add ginger, garlic and green chillies. Add baking soda and salt too.

3) Let it stand for 2 hours before use. Add beaten egg and mix properly.

4) Make pancakes using non-stick pan/tava smeared with little oil.

5) Keep them warm in a casserole. 12 pancakes will be prepared.

For Mushroom Stuffing

Spring onions with greens	6 nos
Tomatoes	3 nos
Green chillies	4 nos
Coriander	¼ cup
Soya sauce	1 tbsp
Chilli powder	¼ tsp
Garam masala	½ tsp
Mushrooms	200 gm
Bread slices	2 nos
Tomato sauce/green chutney	½ cup
Oil for cooking	

Preparation

1) Chop spring onions with the greens, mushrooms, green chillies and coriander very finely. Make crumbs from bread slices.

2) Puree tomatoes (just pass through liquidiser).

3) Heat oil and sauté onions. Add onion greens and chillies. Stir-fry for 2 minutes. Add pureed tomatoes, chilli powder, soya sauce and garam masala. Keep stirring.

4) Add breadcrumbs for binding. Mix well.

5) Add coriander and remove filling from the fire.

Assembly

1) Divide the filling mixture into equal portions.

2) Spread a pancake on chopping board and smear with sauce/chutney and place the filling lengthwise. Roll the pancake. This way finish all the pancakes.

3) Roll the lower portion of each pancake in paper napkin or kitchen foil.

Avoid

Don't add salt to mushroom stuffing; mushrooms have natural salt and soya sauce too flavours it.

Variation

The same stuffing can be used for patties and omelettes. Additional grated cheese can be added.

Preparatory Time: 45 mins

References

1. *Indian Food, A Historical Companion* by Dr K T Achaya
2. *Vegetarian Gourmet Recipes* by Dr Paul C Bragg